Sand and Foam

Kahlil Gibran

CONTENTS

SAND AND FOAM

I am forever walking upon these shores,
Betwixt the sand and the foam,
The high tide will erase my foot-prints,
And the wind will blow away the foam.
But the sea and the shore will remain
Forever.

*

Once I filled my hand with mist.
Then I opened it and lo, the mist was a worm.
And I closed and opened my hand again, and behold there was a bird.
And again I closed and opened my hand, and in its hollow stood a man with a sad face, turned upward.
And again I closed my hand, and when I opened it there was naught but mist.
But I heard a song of exceeding sweetness.

*

It was but yesterday I thought myself a fragment quivering without rhythm in the sphere of life.
Now I know that I am the sphere, and all life in rhythmic fragments moves within me.

*

They say to me in their awakening, "You and the

world you live in are but a grain of sand upon the infinite shore of an infinite sea."

And in my dream I say to them, "I am the infinite sea, and all worlds are but grains of sand upon my shore."

*

Only once have I been made mute. It was when a man asked me, "Who are you?"

*

The first thought of God was an angel.
The first word of God was a man.

*

We were fluttering, wandering, longing creatures a thousand thousand years before the sea and the wind in the forest gave us words.

Now how can we express the ancient of days in us with only the sounds of our yesterdays?

*

The Sphinx spoke only once, and the Sphinx said, "A grain of sand is a desert, and a desert is a grain of sand; and now let us all be silent again."

I heard the Sphinx, but I did not understand.

*

Long did I lie in the dust of Egypt, silent and unaware of the seasons.

Then the sun gave me birth, and I rose and walked upon the banks of the Nile,

Singing with the days and dreaming with the nights.

And now the sun threads upon me with a thousand feet that I may lie again in the dust of Egypt.

But behold a marvel and a riddle!

The very sun that gathered me cannot scatter me.

Still erect am I, and sure of foot do I walk upon the banks of the Nile.

*

Remembrance is a form of meeting.

*

Forgetfulness is a form of freedom.

*

We measure time according to the movement of countless suns; and they measure time by little machines in their little pockets.

Now tell me, how could we ever meet at the same place and the same time?

*

Space is not space between the earth and the sun to one who looks down from the windows of the Milky Way.

*

Humanity is a river of light running from the ex-eternity to eternity.

*

Do not the spirits who dwell in the ether envy man his pain?

*

On my way to the Holy City I met another pilgrim and I asked him, "Is this indeed the way to the Holy City?"

And he said, "Follow me, and you will reach the Holy City in a day and a night."

And I followed him. And we walked many days and many nights, yet we did not reach the Holy City.

And what was to my surprise he became angry with me because he had misled me.

*

Make me, oh God, the prey of the lion, ere You make the rabbit my prey.

*

One may not reach the dawn save by the path of the night.

*

My house says to me, "Do not leave me, for here dwells your past."

And the road says to me, "Come and follow me, for I am your future."

And I say to both my house and the road, "I have no past, nor have I a future. If I stay here, there is a going in my staying; and if I go there is a staying in my going. Only love and death will change all things."

*

4

How can I lose faith in the justice of life, when the dreams of those who sleep upon feathers are not more beautiful than the dreams of those who sleep upon the earth? Strange, the desire for certain pleasures is a part of my pain.

*

Seven times have I despised my soul:
The first time when I saw her being meek that she might attain height.
The second time when I saw her limping before the crippled.
The third time when she was given to choose between the hard and the easy, and she chose the easy.
The fourth time when she committed a wrong, and comforted herself that others also commit wrong.
The fifth time when she forbore for weakness, and attributed her patience to strength.
The sixth time when she despised the ugliness of a face, and knew not that it was one of her own masks.
And the seventh time when she sang a song of praise, and deemed it a virtue.

*

I am ignorant of absolute truth. But I am humble before my ignorance and therein lies my honor and my reward.

*

There is a space between man's imagination and man's attainment that may only be traversed by his longing.

*

Paradise is there, behind that door, in the next room; but I have lost the key.

Perhaps I have only mislaid it.

*

You are blind and I am deaf and dumb, so let us touch hands and understand.

*

The significance of man is not in what he attains, but rather in what he longs to attain.

*

Some of us are like ink and some like paper.

And if it were not for the blackness of some of us, some of us would be dumb;

And if it were not for the whiteness of some of us, some of us would be blind.

*

Give me an ear and I will give you a voice.

*

Our mind is a sponge; our heart is a stream.

Is it not strange that most of us choose sucking rather than running?

*

When you long for blessings that you may not name, and when you grieve knowing not the cause, then indeed you are growing with all things that grow, and rising toward your greater self.

*

When one is drunk with a vision, he deems his faint expression of it the very wine.

*

You drink wine that you may be intoxicated; and I drink that it may sober me from that other wine.

*

When my cup is empty I resign myself to its emptiness; but when it is half full I resent its half-fulness.

*

The reality of the other person is not in what he reveals to you, but in what he cannot reveal to you.
Therefore, if you would understand him, listen not to what he says but rather to what he does not say.

*

Half of what I say is meaningless; but I say it so that the other half may reach you.

*

A sense of humour is a sense of proportion.

*

My loneliness was born when men praised my talkative faults and blamed my silent virtues.

*

When Life does not find a singer to sing her heart she produces a philosopher to speak her mind.

*

A truth is to be known always, to be uttered sometimes.

*

The real in us is silent; the acquired is talkative.

*

The voice of life in me cannot reach the ear of life in you; but let us talk that we may not feel lonely.

*

When two women talk they say nothing; when one woman speaks she reveals all of life.

*

Frogs may bellow louder than bulls, but they cannot drag the plough in the field not turn the wheel of the winepress, and of their skins you cannot make shoes.

*

Only the dumb envy the talkative.

*

If winter should say, "Spring is in my heart," who would believe winter?

*

Every seed is a longing.

*

Should you really open your eyes and see, you would behold your image in all images.
And should you open your ears and listen, you would hear your own voice in all voices.

*

It takes two of us to discover truth: one to utter it and one to understand it.

*

Though the wave of words is forever upon us, yet our depth is forever silent.

*

Many a doctrine is like a window pane. We see truth through it but it divides us from truth.

*

Now let us play hide and seek. Should you hide in my heart it would not be difficult to find you. But should you hide behind your own shell, then it would be useless for anyone to seek you. A woman may veil her face with a smile.

*

How noble is the sad heart who would sing a joyous song with joyous hearts.

*

He who would understand a woman, or dissect genius, or solve the mystery of silence is the very man who would wake from a beautiful dream to sit at a breakfast table.

*

I would walk with all those who walk. I would not stand still to watch the procession passing by.

*

You owe more than gold to him who serves you. Give him of your heart or serve him.

*

Nay, we have not lived in vain. Have they not built towers of our bones?

*

Let us not be particular and sectional. The poet's mind and the scorpion's tail rise in glory from the same earth.

*

Every dragon gives birth to a St. George who slays it.

*

Trees are poems that the earth writes upon the sky.

We fell them down and turn them into paper that we may record our emptiness.

*

Should you care to write (and only the saints know why you should) you must needs have knowledge and art and music — the knowledge of the music of words, the art of being artless, and the magic of loving your readers.

*

They dip their pens in our hearts and think they are inspired.

*

Should a tree write its autobiography it would not be unlike the history of a race.

*

If I were to choose between the power of writing a poem and the ecstasy of a poem unwritten, I would choose the ecstasy. It is better poetry.
But you and all my neighbors agree that I always choose badly.

*

Poetry is not an opinion expressed. It is a song that rises from a bleeding wound or a smiling mouth.

Words are timeless. You should utter them or write them with a knowledge of their timelessness.

*

A poet is a dethroned king sitting among the ashes of his palace trying to fashion an image out of the ashes.

*

Poetry is a deal of joy and pain and wonder, with a dash of the dictionary.

*

In vain shall a poet seek the mother of the songs of his heart.

*

Once I said to a poet, "We shall not know your worth until you die."
And he answered saying, "Yes, death is always the revealer. And if indeed you would know my worth it is that I have more in my heart than upon my tongue, and more in my desire than in my hand."

*

If you sing of beauty though alone in the heart of the desert you will have an audience.

*

Poetry is wisdom that enchants the heart.
Wisdom is poetry that sings in the mind.
If we could enchant man's heart and at the same time sing in his mind,
Then in truth he would live in the shadow of God.

*

Inspiration will always sing; inspiration will never explain.

*

We often sing lullabies to our children that we ourselves may sleep.

*

All our words are but crumbs that fall down from the feast of the mind.

*

Thinking is always the stumbling stone to poetry.

*

A great singer is he who sings our silences.

*

How can you sing if your mouth be filled with food?
How shall your hand be raised in blessing if it is filled with gold?

*

They say the nightingale pierces his bosom with a thorn when he sings his love song.
So do we all. How else should we sing?

*

Genius is but a robin's song at the beginning of a slow spring.

*

Even the most winged spirit cannot escape physical necessity.

*

A madman is not less a musician than you or myself; only the instrument on which he plays is a little out of tune.

*

The song that lies silent in the heart of a mother sings upon the lips of her child.

*

No longing remains unfulfilled.

*

I have never agreed with my other self wholly. The truth of the matter seems to lie between us.

*

Your other self is always sorry for you. But your other self grows on sorrow; so all is well.

*

There is no struggle of soul and body save in the minds of those whose souls are asleep and whose bodies are out of tune.

*

When you reach the heart of life you shall find beauty in all things, even in the eyes that are blind to beauty.

We live only to discover beauty. All else is a form of waiting.

*

Sow a seed and the earth will yield you a flower. Dream your dream to the sky and it will bring you your beloved.

*

The devil died the very day you were born.
Now you do not have to go through hell to meet an angel.

*

Many a woman borrows a man's heart; very few could possess it.

*

If you would possess you must not claim.

*

When a man's hand touches the hand of a woman they both touch the heart of eternity.

*

Love is the veil between lover and lover.

*

Every man loves two women; the one is the creation of his imagination, and the other is not yet born.

Men who do not forgive women their little faults will never enjoy their great virtues.

*

Love that does not renew itself every day becomes a habit and in turn a slavery.

*

Lovers embrace that which is between them rather than each other.

*

Love and doubt have never been on speaking terms.

*

Love is a word of light, written by a hand of light, upon a page of light.

*

Friendship is always a sweet responsibility, never an opportunity.

*

If you do not understand your friend under all conditions you will never understand him.

*

Your most radiant garment is of the other person's weaving;

You most savory meal is that which you eat at the other person's table;

Your most comfortable bed is in the other person's house.

Now tell me, how can you separate yourself from the other person?

*

Your mind and my heart will never agree until your mind ceases to live in numbers and my heart in the mist.

*

We shall never understand one another until we reduce the language to seven words.

*

How shall my heart be unsealed unless it be broken?

*

Only great sorrow or great joy can reveal your truth.
If you would be revealed you must either dance naked in the sun, or carry your cross.

*

Should nature heed what we say of contentment no river would seek the sea, and no winter would turn to Spring. Should she heed all we say of thrift, how many of us would be breathing this air?

*

You see but your shadow when you turn your back to the sun.

*

You are free before the sun of the day, and free before the stars of the night;
And you are free when there is no sun and no moon and no star.
You are even free when you close your eyes upon all there is.
But you are a slave to him whom you love because you love him,
And a slave to him who loves you because he loves you.

*

We are all beggars at the gate of the temple, and each one of us receives his share of the bounty of the King when he enters the temple, and when he goes out.
But we are all jealous of one another, which is another way of belittling the King.

*

You cannot consume beyond your appetite. The other half of the loaf belongs to the other person, and there should remain a little bread for the chance guest.

*

If it were not for your guests all houses would be graves.

*

Said a gracious wolf to a simple sheep, "Will you not honor our house with a visit?"

And the sheep answered, "We would have been honored to visit your house if it were not in your stomach."

*

I stopped my guest on the threshold and said, "Nay, wipe not your feet as you enter, but as you go out."

*

Generosity is not in giving me that which I need more than you do, but it is in giving me that which you need more than I do.

*

You are indeed charitable when you give, and while giving, turn your face away so that you may not see the shyness of the receiver.

*

The difference between the richest man and the poorest is but a day of hunger and an hour of thirst.

*

We often borrow from our tomorrows to pay our debts to our yesterdays.

*

I too am visited by angels and devils, but I get rid of them.

When it is an angel I pray an old prayer, and he is
bored;

When it is a devil I commit an old sin, and he passes
me by.

*

After all this is not a bad prison; but I do not like this
wall between my cell and the next prisoner's cell;

Yet I assure you that I do not wish to reproach the
warder not the Builder of the prison.

*

Those who give you a serpent when you ask for a
fish, may have nothing but serpents to give. It is then
generosity on their part.

*

Trickery succeeds sometimes, but it always commits
suicide.

*

You are truly a forgiver when you forgive murderers
who never spill blood, thieves who never steal, and liars
who utter no falsehood.

*

He who can put his finger upon that which divides
good from evil is he who can touch the very hem of the
garment of God.

*

If your heart is a volcano how shall you expect flowers to bloom in your hands?

*

A strange form of self-indulgence! There are times when I would be wronged and cheated, that I may laugh at the expense of those who think I do not know I am being wronged and cheated.

*

What shall I say of him who is the pursuer playing the part of the pursued?

*

Let him who wipes his soiled hands with your garment take your garment. He may need it again; surely you would not.

*

It is a pity that money-changers cannot be good gardeners.

*

Please do not whitewash your inherent faults with your acquired virtues. I would have the faults; they are like mine own.

*

How often have I attributed to myself crimes I have never committed, so that the other person may feel comfortable in my presence.

21

Even the masks of life are masks of deeper mystery.

*

You may judge others only according to your
knowledge of yourself.
Tell me now, who among us is guilty and who is
unguilty?

*

The truly just is he who feels half guilty of your
misdeeds.

*

Only an idiot and a genius break man-made laws; and
they are the nearest to the heart of God.

*

It is only when you are pursued that you become
swift.

*

I have no enemies, O God, but if I am to have an
enemy
Let his strength be equal to mine,
That truth alone may be the victor.

*

You will be quite friendly with your enemy when you
both die.

*

22

Perhaps a man may commit suicide in self-defense.

*

Long ago there lived a Man who was crucified for being too loving and too lovable.

And strange to relate I met him thrice yesterday.

The first time He was asking a policeman not to take a prostitute to prison; the second time He was drinking wine with an outcast; and the third time He was having a fist-fight with a promoter inside a church.

*

If all they say of good and evil were true, then my life is but one long crime.

*

Pity is but half justice.

*

The only one who has been unjust to me is the one to whose brother I have been unjust.

*

When you see a man led to prison say in your heart, "Mayhap he is escaping from a narrower prison."

And when you see a man drunken say in your heart, "Mayhap he sought escape from something still more unbeautiful."

*

Oftentimes I have hated in self-defense; but if I were stronger I would not have used such a weapon.

*

How stupid is he who would patch the hatred in his eyes with the smile of his lips.

*

Only those beneath me can envy or hate me.

I have never been envied nor hated; I am above no one.

Only those above me can praise or belittle me.

I have never been praised nor belittled; I am below no one.

*

Your saying to me, "I do not understand you," is praise beyond my worth, and an insult you do not deserve. How mean am I when life gives me gold and I give you silver, and yet I deem myself generous.

*

When you reach the heart of life you will find yourself not higher than the felon, and not lower than the prophet.

*

Strange that you should pity the slow-footed and not the slow-minded,

And the blind-eyed rather than the blind-hearted.

*

It is wiser for the lame not to break his crutches upon the head of his enemy.

*

How blind is he who gives you out of his pocket that he may take out of your heart.

*

Life is a procession. The slow of foot finds it too swift and he steps out;
And the swift of foot finds it too slow and he too steps out.

*

If there is such a thing as sin some of us commit it backward following our forefathers' footsteps;
And some of us commit it forward by overruling our children.

*

The truly good is he who is one with all those who are deemed bad.

*

We are all prisoners but some of us are in cells with windows and some without.

*

Strange that we all defend our wrongs with more vigor than we do our rights

Should we all confess our sins to one another we would all laugh at one another for our lack of originality.

Should we all reveal our virtues we would also laugh for the same cause.

*

An individual is above man-made laws until he commits a crime against man-made conventions; After that he is neither above anyone nor lower than anyone.

*

Government is an agreement between you and myself. You and myself are often wrong.

*

Crime is either another name of need or an aspect of a disease.

*

Is there a greater fault than being conscious of the other person's faults?

*

If the other person laughs at you, you can pity him; but if you laugh at him you may never forgive yourself.

If the other person injures you, you may forget the injury; but if you injure him you will always remember.

In truth the other person is your most sensitive self given another body.

*

How heedless you are when you would have men fly
with your wings and you cannot even give them a feather.

*

Once a man sat at my board and ate my bread and
drank my wine and went away laughing at me.
Then he came again for bread and wine, and I spurned
him;
And the angels laughed at me.

*

Hate is a dead thing. Who of you would be a tomb?

*

It is the honor of the murdered that he is not the
murderer.

*

The tribune of humanity is in its silent heart, never its
talkative mind.

*

They deem me mad because I will not sell my days for
gold;
And I deem them mad because they think my days
have a price.

*

They spread before us their riches of gold and silver,

of ivory and ebony, and we spread before them our hearts and our spirits.;

And yet they deem themselves the hosts and us the guests.

*

I would not be the least among men with dreams and the desire to fulfill them, rather than the greatest with no dreams and no desires.

*

The most pitiful among men is he who turns his dreams into silver and gold.

*

We are all climbing toward the summit of our hearts' desire. Should the other climber steal your sack and your purse and wax fat on the one and heavy on the other, you should pity him;

The climbing will be harder for his flesh, and the burden will make his way longer.

And should you in your leanness see his flesh puffing upward, help him a step; it will add to your swiftness.

*

You cannot judge any man beyond your knowledge of him, and how small is your knowledge.

*

I would not listen to a conqueror preaching to the conquered.

*

The truly free man is he who bears the load of the bond slave patiently.

*

A thousand years ago my neighbor said to me, "I hate life, for it is naught but a thing of pain."

And yesterday I passed by a cemetery and saw life dancing upon his grave.

*

Strife in nature is but disorder longing for order.

*

Solitude is a silent storm that breaks down all our dead branches;

Yet it sends our living roots deeper into the living heart of the living earth.

*

Once I spoke of the sea to a brook, and the brook thought me but an imaginative exaggerator;

And once I spoke of a brook to the sea, and the sea thought me but a depreciative defamer.

*

How narrow is the vision that exalts the busyness of the ant above the singing of the grasshopper.

*

The highest virtue here may be the least in another world.

*

The deep and the high go to the depth or to the height in a straight line; only the spacious can move in circles.

*

If it were not for our conception of weights and measures we would stand in awe of the firefly as we do before the sun.

*

A scientist without imagination is a butcher with dull knives and out-worn scales.
But what would you, since we are not all vegetarians?

*

When you sing the hungry hears you with his stomach.

*

Death is not nearer to the aged than to the new-born; neither is life.

*

If indeed you must be candid, be candid beautifully; otherwise keep silent, for there is a man in our neighborhood who is dying.

*

Mayhap a funeral among men is a wedding feast among the angels.

*

A forgotten reality may die and leave in its will seven thousand actualities and facts to be spent in its funeral and the building of a tomb.

*

In truth we talk only to ourselves, but sometimes we talk loud enough that others may hear us.

*

The obvious is that which is never seen until someone expresses it simply.

*

If the Milky Way were not within me how should I have seen it or known it?

*

Unless I am a physician among physicians they would not believe that I am an astronomer.

*

Perhaps the sea's definition of a shell is the pearl. Perhaps time's definition of coal is the diamond.

*

Fame is the shadow of passion standing in the light.

*

A root is a flower that disdains fame.

There is neither religion nor science beyond beauty.

*

Every great man I have known had something small in his make-up; and it was that small something which prevented inactivity or madness or suicide.

*

The truly great man is he who would master no one, and who would be mastered by none.

*

I would not believe that a man is mediocre simply because he kills the criminals and the prophets.

*

Tolerance is love sick with the sickness of haughtiness.

*

Worms will turn; but is it not strange that even elephants will yield?

*

A disagreement may be the shortest cut between two minds.

*

I am the flame and I am the dry bush, and one part of me consumes the other part.

We are all seeking the summit of the holy moutain; but shall not our road be shorter if we consider the past a chart and not a guide?

*

Wisdom ceases to be wisdom when it becomes too proud to weep, too grave to laugh, and too self-ful to seek other than itself.

*

Had I filled myself with all that you know what room should I have for all that you do not know?

*

I have learned silence from the talkative, toleration from the intolerant, and kindness from the unkind; yet strange, I am ungrateful to these teachers.

*

A bigot is a stone-leaf orator.

*

The silence of the envious is too noisy.

*

When you reach the end of what you should know, you will be at the beginning of what you should sense.

*

An exaggeration is a truth that has lost its temper.

If you can see only what light reveals and hear only what sound announces,
Then in truth you do not see nor do you hear.

*

A fact is a truth unsexed.

*

You cannot laugh and be unkind at the same time.

*

The nearest to my heart are a king without a kingdom and a poor man who does not know how to beg.

*

A shy failure is nobler than an immodest success.

*

Dig anywhere in the earth and you will find a treasure, only you must dig with the faith of a peasant.

*

Said a hunted fox followed by twenty horsemen and a pack of twenty hounds, "Of course they will kill me. But how poor and how stupid they must be. Surely it would not be worth while for twenty foxes riding on twenty asses and accompanied by twenty wolves to chase and kill one man."

*

It is the mind in us that yields to the laws made by us,
but never the spirit in us.

*

A traveler am I and a navigator, and every day I
discover a new region within my soul.

*

A woman protested saying, "Of course it was a
righteous war. My son fell in it."

*

I said to Life, "I would hear Death speak."
And Life raised her voice a little higher and said, "You
hear him now."

*

When you have solved all the mysteries of life you
long for death, for it is but another mystery of life.

*

Birth and death are the two noblest expressions of
bravery.

*

My friend, you and I shall remain strangers unto life,
And unto one another, and each unto himself,
Until the day when you shall speak and I shall listen
Deeming your voice my own voice;
And when I shall stand before you
Thinking myself standing before a mirror.

*

They say to me, "Should you know yourself you would know all men."

And I say, "Only when I seek all men shall I know myself."

*

Man is two men; one is awake in darkness, the other is asleep in light.

*

A hermit is one who renounces the world of fragments that he may enjoy the world wholly and without interruption.

*

There lies a green field between the scholar and the poet; should the scholar cross it he becomes a wise man; should the poet cross it, he becomes a prophet.

*

Yestereve I saw philosophers in the market-place carrying their heads in baskets, and crying aloud, "Wisdom! Wisdom for sale!"

Poor philosophers! They must needs sell their heads to feed their hearts. Said a philosopher to a street sweeper, "I pity you. Yours is a hard and dirty task."

And the street sweeper said, "Thank you, sir. But tell me what is your task?"

And the philosopher answered saying, "I study man's mind, his deeds and his desires."

Then the street sweeper went on with his sweeping and said with a smile, "I pity you too."

*

He who listens to truth is not less than he who utters truth.

*

No man can draw the line between necessities and luxuries. Only the angels can do that, and the angels are wise and wistful.
Perhaps the angels are our better thought in space.

*

He is the true prince who finds his throne in the heart of the dervish.

*

Generosity is giving more than you can, and pride is taking less than you need.

*

In truth you owe naught to any man. You owe all to all men.

*

All those who have lived in the past live with us now. Surely none of us would be an ungracious host.

*

He who longs the most lives the longest.

*

They say to me, "A bird in the hand is worth ten in the bush."

But I say, "A bird and a feather in the bush is worth more than ten birds in the hand."

Your seeking after that feather is life with winged feet; nay, it is life itself.

*

There are only two elements here, beauty and truth; beauty in the hearts of lovers, and truth in the arms of the tillers of the soil.

*

Great beauty captures me, but a beauty still greater frees me even from itself.

*

Beauty shines brighter in the heart of him who longs for it than in the eyes of him who sees it.

*

I admire him who reveals his mind to me; I honor him who unveils his dreams. But why am I shy, and even a little ashamed before him who serves me?

*

The gifted were once proud in serving princes.
Now they claim honor in serving paupers.

38

The angels know that too many practical men eat their bread with the sweat of the dreamer's brow.

*

Wit is often a mask. If you could tear it you would find either a genius irritated or cleverness juggling.

*

The understanding attributes to me understanding and the dull, dullness. I think they are both right.

*

Only those with secrets in their hearts could divine the secrets in our hearts.

*

He who would share your pleasure but not your pain shall lose the key to one of the seven gates of Paradise.

*

Yes, there is a Nirvanah; it is in leading your sheep to a green pasture, and in putting your child to sleep, and in writing the last line of your poem.

*

We choose our joys and our sorrows long before we experience them.

*

Sadness is but a wall between two gardens.

*

When either your joy or your sorrow becomes great the world becomes small.

*

Desire is half of life; idifference is half of death.

*

The bitterest thing in our today's sorrow is the memory of our yesterday's joy.

*

They say to me, "You must needs choose between the pleasures of this world and the peace of the next world."
And I say to them, "I have chosen both the delights of this world and the peace of the next. For I know in my heart that the Supreme Poet wrote but one poem, and it scans perfectly, and it also rhymes perfectly."

*

Faith is an oasis in the heart which will never be reached by the caravan of thinking.

*

When you reach your height you shall desire but only for desire; and you shall hunger, for hunger; and you shall thirst for greater thirst.

*

If you reveal your secrets to the wind you should not blame the wind for revealing them to the trees.

*

The flowers of spring are winter's dreams related at the breakfast table of the angels.

*

Said a skunk to a tube-rose, "See how swiftly I run, while you cannot walk nor even creep."
Said the tube-rose to the skunk, "Oh, most noble swift runner, please run swiftly!"

*

Turtles can tell more about roads than hares.

*

Strange that creatures without backbones have the hardest shells.

*

The most talkative is the least intelligent, and there is hardly a difference between an orator and an auctioneer.

*

Be grateful that you do not have to live down the renown of a father nor the wealth of an uncle.
But above all be grateful that no one will have to live down either your renown or your wealth.

*

Only when a juggler misses catching his ball does he appeal to me.

*

The envious praises me unknowingly.

*

Long were you a dream in your mother's sleep, and then she woke to give you birth.

*

The germ of the race is in your mother's longing.

*

My father and mother desired a child and they begot me.

And I wanted a mother and a father and I begot night and the sea.

*

Some of our children are our justifications and some are but our regrets.

*

When night comes and you too are dark, lie down and be dark with a will.

And when morning comes and you are still dark stand up and say to the day with a will, "I am still dark."

It is stupid to play a role with the night and the day.

They would both laugh at you.

*

The mountain veiled in mist is not a hill; an oak tree in the rain is not a weeping willow.

*

Behold here is a paradox; the deep and high are nearer to one another than the mid-level to either.

*

When I stood a clear mirror before you, you gazed into me and saw your image.
Then you said, "I love you."
But in truth you loved yourself in me.

*

When you enjoy loving your neighbor it ceases to be a virtue.

*

Love which is not always springing is always dying.

*

You cannot have youth and the knowledge of it at the same time;
For youth is too busy living to know, and knowledge is too busy seeking itself to live. You may sit at your window watching the passersby. And watching you may see a nun walking toward your right hand, and a prostitute toward your left hand.
And you may say in your innocence, "How noble is the one and how ignoble is the other."

But should you close your eyes and listen awhile you would hear a voice whispering in the ether, "One seeks me in prayer, and the other in pain. And in the spirit of each there is a bower for my spirit."

*

Once every hundred years Jesus of Nazareth meets Jesus of the Christian in a garden among the hills of Lebanon. And they talk long; and each time Jesus of Nazareth goes away saying to Jesus of the Christian, "My friend, I fear we shall never, never agree."

*

May God feed the over-abundant!

*

A great man has two hearts; one bleeds and the other forbears.

*

Should one tell a lie which does not hurt you nor anyone else, why not say in your heart that the house of his facts is too small for his fancies, and he had to leave it for larger space?

*

Behind every closed door is a mystery sealed with seven seals.

*

Waiting is the hoofs of time.

44

What if trouble should be a new window in the Eastern wall of your house?

*

You may forget the one with whom you have laughed, but never the one with whom you have wept.

*

There must be something strangely sacred in salt. It is in our tears and in the sea.

*

Our God in His gracious thirst will drink us all, the dewdrop and the tear.

*

You are but a fragment of your giant self, a mouth that seeks bread, and a blind hand that holds the cup for a thirsty mouth.

*

If you would rise but a cubit above race and country and self you would indeed become godlike.

*

If I were you I would not find fault with the sea at low tide.
It is a good ship and our Captain is able; it is only your stomach that is in disorder.

*

Should you sit upon a cloud you would not see the boundary line between one country and another, nor the boundary stone between a farm and a farm.

It is a pity you cannot sit upon a cloud.

*

Seven centuries ago seven white doves rose from a deep valley flying to the snow-white summit of the mountain. One of the seven men who watched the flight said, "I see a black spot on the wing of the seventh dove."

Today the people in that valley tell of seven black doves who flew to the summit of the snowy mountain.

*

In the autumn I gathered all my sorrows and buried them in my garden.

And when April returned and spring came to wed the earth, there grew in my garden beautiful flowers unlike all other flowers.

And my neighbors came to behold them, and they all said to me, "When autumn comes again, at seeding time, will you not give us of the seeds of these flowers that we may have them in our gardens?"

*

It is indeed misery if I stretch an empty hand to men and receive nothing; but it is hopelessness if I stretch a full hand and find none to receive.

*

I long for eternity because there I shall meet my unwritten poems and my unpainted pictures.

Art is a step from nature toward the Infinite.

*

A work of art is a mist carved into an image.

*

Even the hands that make crowns of thorns are better than idle hands.

*

Our most sacred tears never seek our eyes.

*

Every man is the descendant of every king and every slave that ever lived.

*

If the great-grandfather of Jesus had known what was hidden within him, would he not have stood in awe of himself?

*

Was the love of Judas' mother of her son less than the love of Mary for Jesus?

*

There are three miracles of our Brother Jesus not yet recorded in the Book: the first that He was a man like you and me, the second that He had a sense of humour, and the third that He knew He was a conqueror though conquered.

Crucified One, you are crucified upon my heart; and the nails that pierce your hands pierce the walls of my heart.

And tomorrow when a stranger passes by this Golgotha he will not know that two bled here.

He will deem it the blood of one man.

*

You may have heard of the Blessed Mountain.

It is the highest mountain in our world.

Should you reach the summit you would have only one desire, and that to descend and be with those who dwell in the deepest valley.

That is why it is called the Blessed Mountain.

*

Every thought I have imprisoned in expression I must free by my deeds.

THE MADMAN
HIS PARABLES AND POEMS

You ask me how I became a madman. It happened thus: One day, long before many gods were born, I woke from a deep sleep and found all my masks were stolen,—the seven masks I have fashioned and worn in seven lives,—I ran maskless through the crowded streets shouting, "Thieves, thieves, the cursed thieves."

Men and women laughed at me and some ran to their houses in fear of me.

And when I reached the market place, a youth standing on a house-top cried, "He is a madman." I looked up to behold him; the sun kissed my own naked face for the first time. For the first time the sun kissed my own naked face and my soul was inflamed with love for the sun, and I wanted my masks no more. And as if in a trance I cried, "Blessed, blessed are the thieves who stole my masks."

Thus I became a madman.

And I have found both freedom and safety in my madness; the freedom of loneliness and the safety from being understood, for those who understand us enslave something in us.

But let me not be too proud of my safety. Even a Thief in a jail is safe from another thief.

GOD

In the ancient days, when the first quiver of speech came to my lips, I ascended the holy mountain and spoke unto God, saying, "Master, I am thy slave. Thy hidden will is my law and I shall obey thee for ever more."

But God made no answer, and like a mighty tempest passed away.

And after a thousand years I ascended the holy mountain and again spoke unto God, saying, "Creator, I am thy creation. Out of clay hast thou fashioned me and to thee I owe mine all."

And God made no answer, but like a thousand swift wings passed away.

And after a thousand years I climbed the holy mountain and spoke unto God again, saying, "Father, I am thy son. In pity and love thou hast given me birth, and through love and worship I shall inherit thy kingdom."

And God made no answer, and like the mist that veils the distant hills he passed away.

And after a thousand years I climbed the sacred mountain and again spoke unto God, saying, "My God, my aim and my fulfillment; I am thy yesterday and thou are my tomorrow. I am thy root in the earth and thou art my flower in the sky, and together we grow before the face of the sun."

Then God leaned over me, and in my ears whispered words of sweetness, and even as the sea that enfoldeth a brook that runneth down to her, he enfolded me.

And when I descended to the valleys and the plains God was there also.

MY FRIEND

My friend, I am not what I seem. Seeming is but a garment I wear—a care-woven garment that protects me from thy questionings and thee from my negligence.

The "I" in me, my friend, dwells in the house of

silence, and therein it shall remain for ever more, unperceived, unapproachable.

I would not have thee believe in what I say nor trust in what I do—for my words are naught but thy own thoughts in sound and my deeds thy own hopes in action.

When thou sayest, "The wind bloweth eastward," I say, "Aye it doth blow eastward"; for I would not have thee know that my mind doth not dwell upon the wind but upon the sea.

Thou canst not understand my seafaring thoughts, nor would I have thee understand. I would be at sea alone.

When it is day with thee, my friend, it is night with me; yet even then I speak of the noontide that dances upon the hills and of the purple shadow that steals its way across the valley; for thou canst not hear the songs of my darkness nor see my wings beating against the stars—and I fain would not have thee hear or see. I would be with night alone.

When thou ascendest to thy Heaven I descend to my Hell—even then thou callest to me across the unbridgeable gulf, "My companion, my comrade," and I call back to thee, "My comrade, my companion"—for I would not have thee see my Hell. The flame would burn thy eyesight and the smoke would crowd thy nostrils. And I love my Hell too well to have thee visit it. I would be in Hell alone.

Thou lovest Truth and Beauty and Righteousness; and I for thy sake say it is well and seemly to love these things. But in my heart I laught at thy love. Yet I would not have thee see my laughter. I would laugh alone.

My friend, thou art good and cautious and wise; nay, thou art perfect—and I, too, speak with thee wisely and cautiously. And yet I am mad. But I mask my madness. I would be mad alone.

My friend, thou art not my friend, but how shall I

make thee understand? My path is not thy path, yet together we walk, hand in hand.

THE SCARECROW

Once I said to a scarecrow, "You must be tired of standing in this lonely field."

And he said, "The joy of scaring is a deep and lasting one, and I never tire of it."

Said I, after a minute of thought, "It is true; for I too have known that joy."

Said he, "Only those who are stuffed with straw can know it."

Then I left him, not knowing whether he had complimented or belittled me.

A year passed, during which the scarecrow turned philosopher.

And when I passed by him again I saw two crows building a nest under his hat.

THE SLEEP-WALKERS

In the town where I was born lived a woman and her daughter, who walked in their sleep.

One night, while silence enfolded the world, the woman and her daughter, walking, yet asleep, met in their mist-veiled garden.

And the mother spoke, and she said: "At last, at last, my enemy! You by whom my youth was destroyed—who have built up your life upon the ruins of mine! Would I could kill you!"

And the daughter spoke, and she said: "O hateful woman, selfish and old! Who stand between my freer self and me! Who would have my life an echo of your own faded life! Would you were dead!"

At that moment a cock crew, and both women awoke. The mother said gently, "Is that you, darling?" And the daughter answered gently, "Yes, dear."

THE WISE DOG

One day there passed by a company of cats a wise dog.

And as he came near and saw that they were very intent and heeded him not, he stopped.

Then there arose in the midst of the company a large, grave cat and looked upon them and said, "Brethren, pray ye; and when ye have prayed again and yet again, nothing doubting, verily then it shall rain mice."

And when the dog heard this he laughed in his heart and turned from them saying, "O blind and foolish cats, has it not been written and have I not known and my fathers before me, that that which raineth for prayer and faith and supplication is not mice but bones."

THE TWO HERMITS

Upon a lonely mountain, there lived two hermits who worshipped God and loved one another.

Now these two hermits had one earthen bowl, and this was their only possession.

One day an evil spirit entered into the heart of the older hermit and he came to the younger and said, "It is long that we have lived together. The time has come for us to part. Let us divide our possessions."

Then the younger hermit was saddened and he said, "It grieves me, Brother, that thou shouldst leave me. But if thou must needs go, so be it," and he brought the earthen bowl and gave it to him saying, "We cannot divide it, Brother, let it be thine."

Then the older hermit said, "Charity I will not accept. I will take nothing but mine own. It must be divided."

And the younger one said, "If the bowl be broken, of what use would it be to thee or to me? If it be thy pleasure let us rather cast a lot."

But the older hermit said again, "I will have but justice and mine own, and I will not trust justice and mine own to vain chance. The bowl must be divided."

Then the younger hermit could reason no further and he said, "If it be indeed thy will, and if even so thou wouldst have it let us now break the bowl."

But the face of the older hermit grew exceedingly dark, and he cried, "O thou cursed coward, thou wouldst not fight."

ON GIVING AND TAKING

Once there lived a man who had a valley-full of needles. And one day the mother of Jesus came to him and said: "Friend, my son's garment is torn and I must needs mend it before he goeth to the temple. Wouldst thou not give me a needle?"

And he gave her not a needle, but he gave her a
learned discourse on Giving and Taking to carry to her
son before he should go to the temple.

THE SEVEN SELVES

In the stillest hour of the night, as I lay half asleep, my
seven selves sat together and thus conversed in whisper:

First Self: Here, in this madman, I have dwelt all these
years, with naught to do but renew his pain by day and
recreate his sorrow by night. I can bear my fate no longer,
and now I rebel.

Second Self: Yours is a better lot than mine, brother,
for it is given to me to be this madman's joyous self. I
laugh his laughter and sing his happy hours, and with
thrice winged feet I dance his brighter thoughts. It is I that
would rebel against my weary existence.

Third Self: And what of me, the love-ridden self, the
flaming brand of wild passion and fantastic desires? It is I
the love-sick self who would rebel against this madman.

Fourth Self: I, amongst you all, am the most miserable,
for naught was given me but odious hatred and destructive
loathing. It is I, the tempest-like self, the one born in the
black caves of Hell, who would protest against serving
this madman.

Fifth Self: Nay, it is I, the thinking self, the fanciful
self, the self of hunger and thirst, the one doomed to
wander without rest in search of unknown things and
things not yet created; it is I, not you, who would rebel.

Sixth Self: And I, the working self, the pitiful
labourer, who, with patient hands, and longing eyes,
fashion the days into images and give the formless

elements new and eternal forms—it is I, the solitary one, who would rebel against this restless madman.

Seventh Self: How strange that you all would rebel against this man, because each and every one of you has a preordained fate to fulfill. Ah! could I but be like one of you, a self with a determined lot! But I have none, I am the do-nothing self, the one who sits in the dumb, empty nowhere and nowhen, while you are busy re-creating life. Is it you or I, neighbours, who should rebel?

When the seventh self thus spake the other six selves looked with pity upon him but said nothing more; and as the night grew deeper one after the other went to sleep enfolded with a new and happy submission.

But the seventh self remained watching and gazing at nothingness, which is behind all things.

WAR

One night a feast was held in the palace, and there came a man and prostrated himself before the prince, and all the feasters looked upon him; and they saw that one of his eyes was out and that the empty socket bled. And the prince inquired of him, "What has befallen you?" And the man replied, "O prince, I am by profession a thief, and this night, because there was no moon, I went to rob the money-changer's shop, and as I climbed in through the window I made a mistake and entered the weaver's shop, and in the dark I ran into the weaver's loom and my eye was plucked out. And now, O prince, I ask for justice upon the weaver."

Then the prince sent for the weaver and he came, and it was decreed that one of his eyes should be plucked out.

"O prince," said the weaver, "the decree is just. It is

right that one of my eyes be taken. And yet, alas! both are
necessary to me in order that I may see the two sides of
the cloth that I weave. But I have a neighbour, a cobbler,
who has also two eyes, and in his trade both eyes are not
necessary."

Then the prince sent for the cobbler. And he came.
And they took out one of the cobbler's two eyes.

And justice was satisfied.

THE FOX

A fox looked at his shadow at sunrise and said, "I will
have a camel for lunch today." And all morning he went
about looking for camels. But at noon he saw his shadow
again—and he said, "A mouse will do."

THE WISE KING

Once there ruled in the distant city of Wirani a king
who was both mighty and wise. And he was feared for his
might and loved for his wisdom.

Now, in the heart of that city was a well, whose water
was cool and crystalline, from which all the inhabitants
drank, even the king and his courtiers; for there was no
other well.

One night when all were asleep, a witch entered the
city, and poured seven drops of strange liquid into the
well, and said, "From this hour he who drinks this water
shall become mad."

Next morning all the inhabitants, save the king and

his lord chamberlain, drank from the well and became mad, even as the witch had foretold.

And during that day the people in the narrow streets and in the market places did naught but whisper to one another, "The king is mad. Our king and his lord chamberlain have lost their reason. Surely we cannot be ruled by a mad king. We must dethrone him."

That evening the king ordered a golden goblet to be filled from the well. And when it was brought to him he drank deeply, and gave it to his lord chamberlain to drink.

And there was great rejoicing in that distant city of Wirani, because its king and its lord chamberlain had regained their reason.

AMBITION

Three men met at a tavern table. One was a weaver, another a carpenter and the third a ploughman.

Said the weaver, "I sold a fine linen shroud today for two pieces of gold. Let us have all the wine we want."

"And I," said the carpenter, "I sold my best coffin. We will have a great roast with the wine."

"I only dug a grave," said the ploughman, "but my patron paid me double. Let us have honey cakes too."

And all that evening the tavern was busy, for they called often for wine and meat and cakes. And they were merry.

And the host rubbed his hands and smiled at his wife; for his guests were spending freely.

When they left the moon was high, and they walked along the road singing and shouting together.

The host and his wife stood in the tavern door and looked after them.

"Ah!" said the wife, "these gentlemen! So freehanded and so gay! If only they could bring us such luck every day! Then our son need not be a tavern-keeper and work so hard. We could educate him, and he could become a priest."

THE NEW PLEASURE

Last night I invented a new pleasure, and as I was giving it the first trial an angel and a devil came rushing toward my house. They met at my door and fought with each other over my newly created pleasure; the one crying, "It is a sin!"—the other, "It is a virtue!"

THE OTHER LANGUAGE

Three days after I was born, as I lay in my silken cradle, gazing with astonished dismay on the new world round about me, my mother spoke to the wet-nurse, saying, "How does my child?"

And the wet-nurse answered, "He does well, Madame, I have fed him three times; and never before have I seen a babe so young yet so gay."

And I was indignant; and I cried, "It is not true, mother; for my bed is hard, and the milk I have sucked is bitter to my mouth, and the odour of the breast is foul in my nostrils, and I am most miserable."

But my mother did not understand, nor did the nurse; for the language I spoke was that of the world from which I came.

And on the twenty-first day of my life, as I was being christened, the priest said to my mother, "You should indeed by happy, Madame, that your son was born a Christian."

And I was surprised,—and I said to the priest, "Then your mother in Heaven should be unhappy, for you were not born a Christian."

But the priest too did not understand my language.

And after seven moons, one day a soothsayer looked at me, and he said to my mother, "Your son will be a statesman and a great leader of men."

But I cried out,—"That is a false prophet; for I shall be a musician, and naught but a musician shall I be."

But even at that age my language was not understood—and great was my astonishment.

And after three and thirty years, during which my mother, and the nurse, and the priest have all died, (the shadow of God be upon their spirits) the soothsayer still lives. And yesterday I met him near the gates of the temple; and while we were talking together he said, "I have always known you would become a great musician. Even in your infancy I prophesied and foretold your future."

And I believed him—for now I too have forgotten the language of that other world.

THE POMEGRANATE

Once when I was living in the heart of a pomegranate, I heard a seed saying, "Someday I shall become a tree, and the wind will sing in my branches, and the sun will dance on my leaves, and I shall be strong and beautiful through all the seasons."

Then another seed spoke and said, "When I was as young as you, I too held such views; but now that I can weigh and measure things, I see that my hopes were vain."

And a third seed spoke also, "I see in us nothing that promises so great a future."

And a fourth said, "But what a mockery our life would be, without a greater future!"

Said a fifth, "Why dispute what we shall be, when we know not even what we are."

But a sixth replied, "Whatever we are, that we shall continue to be."

And a seventh said, "I have such a clear idea how everything will be, but I cannot put it into words."

Then an eight spoke—and a ninth—and a tenth—and then many—until all were speaking, and I could distinguish nothing for the many voices.

And so I moved that very day into the heart of a quince, where the seeds are few and almost silent.

THE TWO CAGES

In my father's garden there are two cages. In one is a lion, which my father's slaves brought from the desert of Ninavah; in the other is a songless sparrow.

Every day at dawn the sparrow calls to the lion, "Good morrow to thee, brother prisoner."

THE THREE ANTS

Three ants met on the nose of a man who was asleep in the sun. And after they had saluted one another, each according to the custom of his tribe, they stood there conversing.

The first ant said, "These hills and plains are the most barren I have known. I have searched all day for a grain of some sort, and there is none to be found."

Said the second ant, "I too have found nothing, though I have visited every nook and glade. This is, I believe, what my people call the soft, moving land where nothing grows."

Then the third ant raised his head and said, "My friends, we are standing now on the nose of the Supreme Ant, the mighty and infinite Ant, whose body is so great that we cannot see it, whose shadow is so vast that we cannot trace it, whose voice is so loud that we cannot hear it; and He is omnipresent."

When the third ant spoke thus the other ants looked at each other and laughed.

At that moment the man moved and in his sleep raised his hand and scratched his nose, and the three ants were crushed.

THE GRAVE-DIGGER

Once, as I was burying one of my dead selves, the grave-digger came by and said to me, "Of all those who come here to bury, you alone I like."

Said I, "You please me exceedingly, but why do you like me?"

"Because," said he, "They come weeping and go weeping—you only come laughing and go laughing."

ON THE STEPS OF THE TEMPLE

Yestereve, on the marble steps of the Temple, I saw a

woman sitting between two men. One side of her face was pale, the other was blushing.

THE BLESSED CITY

In my youth I was told that in a certain city every one lived according to the Scriptures.

And I said, "I will seek that city and the blessedness thereof." And it was far. And I made great provision for my journey. And after forty days I beheld the city and on the forty-first day I entered into it.

And lo! the whole company of the inhabitants had each but a single eye and but one hand. And I was astonished and said to myself, "Shall they of this so holy city have but one eye and one hand?"

Then I saw that they too were astonished, for they were marveling greatly at my two hands and my two eyes. And as they were speaking together I inquired of them saying, "Is this indeed the Blessed City, where each man lives according to the Scriptures?" And they said, "Yes, this is that city."

"And what," said I, "hath befallen you, and where are your right eyes and your right hands?"

And all the people were moved. And they said, "Come thou and see."

And they took me to the temple in the midst of the city. And in the temple I saw a heap of hands and eyes. All withered. Then said I, "Alas! what conqueror hath committed this cruelty upon you?"

And there went a murmur amongst them. And one of their elders stood forth and said, "This doing is of ourselves. God hath made us conquerors over the evil that was in us."

And he led me to a high altar, and all the people
followed. And he showed me above the altar an
inscription graven, and I read:

"If thy right eye offend thee, pluck it out and cast it
from thee; for it is profitable for thee that one of thy
members should perish, and not that the whole body
should be cast into hell. And if thy right hand offend thee,
cut it off and cast it from thee; for it is profitable for thee
that one of thy members should perish, and not that thy
whole body should be cast into hell."

Then I understood. And I turned about to all the people
and cried, "Hath no man or woman among you two eyes or
two hands?"

And they answered me saying, "No, not one. There is
none whole save such as are yet too young to read the
Scripture and to understand its commandment."

And when we had come out of the temple, I
straightway left that Blessed City; for I was not too young,
and I could read the scripture.

THE GOOD GOD AND THE EVIL GOD

The Good God and the Evil God met on the mountain
top.

The Good God said, "Good day to you, brother."

The Evil God did not answer.

And the Good God said, "You are in a bad humour
today."

"Yes," said the Evil God, "for of late I have been often
mistaken for you, called by your name, and treated as if I
were you, and it ill-pleases me."

And the Good God said, "But I too have been mistaken
for you and called by your name."

The Evil God walked away cursing the stupidity of man.

DEFEAT

Defeat, my Defeat, my solitude and my aloofness;
You are dearer to me than a thousand triumphs,
And sweeter to my heart than all world-glory.

Defeat, my Defeat, my self-knowledge and my defiance,
Through you I know that I am yet young and swift of foot
And not to be trapped by withering laurels.
And in you I have found aloneness
And the joy of being shunned and scorned.

Defeat, my Defeat, my shining sword and shield,
In your eyes I have read
That to be enthroned is to be enslaved,
And to be understood is to be leveled down,
And to be grasped is but to reach one's fullness
And like a ripe fruit to fall and be consumed.
Defeat, my Defeat, my bold companion,
You shall hear my songs and my cries and my silences,
And none but you shall speak to me of the beating of wings,
And urging of seas,
And of mountains that burn in the night,
And you alone shall climb my steep and rocky soul.

Defeat, my Defeat, my deathless courage,
You and I shall laugh together with the storm,

And together we shall dig graves for all that die in us,
And we shall stand in the sun with a will,
And we shall be dangerous.

NIGHT AND THE MADMAN

"I am like thee, O, Night, dark and naked; I walk on the flaming path which is above my day-dreams, and whenever my foot touches earth a giant oak tree comes forth."

"Nay, thou art not like me, O, Madman, for thou still lookest backward to see how large a foot-print thou leavest on the sand."

"I am like thee, O, Night, silent and deep; and in the heart of my loneliness lies a Goddess in child-bed; and in him who is being born Heaven touches Hell."

"Nay, thou art not like me, O, Madman, for thou shudderest yet before pain, and the song of the abyss terrifies thee."

"I am like thee, O, Night, wild and terrible; for my ears are crowded with cries of conquered nations and sighs for forgotten lands."

"Nay, thou art not like me, O, Madman, for thou still takest thy little-self for a comrade, and with thy monster-self thou canst not be friend."

"I am like thee, O, Night, cruel and awful; for my bosom is lit by burning ships at sea, and my lips are wet with blood of slain warriors."

"Nay, thou art not like me, O, Madman; for the desire for a sister-spirit is yet upon thee, and thou has not become alone unto thyself."

"I am like thee, O, Night, joyous and glad; for he who

dwells in my shadow is now drunk with virgin wine, and she who follows me is sinning mirthfully."

"Nay, thou art not like me, O, Madman, for thy soul is wrapped in the veil of seven folds and thou holdest not thy heart in thine hand."

"I am like thee, O, Night, patient and passionate; for in my breast a thousand dead lovers are buried in shrouds of withered kisses."

"Yea, Madman, art thou like me? Art thou like me? And canst thou ride the tempest as a steed, and grasp the lightning as a sword?"

"Like thee, O, Night, like thee, mighty and high, and my throne is built upon heaps of fallen Gods; and before me too pass the days to kiss the hem of my garment but never to gaze at my face."

"Art thou like me, child of my darkest heart? And dost thou think my untamed thoughts and speak my vast language?"

"Yea, we are twin brothers, O, Night; for thou revealest space and I reveal my soul."

FACES

I have seen a face with a thousand countenances, and a face that was but a single countenance as if held in a mould.

I have seen a face whose sheen I could look through to the ugliness beneath, and a face whose sheen I had to lift to see how beautiful it was.

I have seen an old face much lined with nothing, and a smooth face in which all things were graven.

I know faces, because I look through the fabric my own eye weaves, and behold the reality beneath.

My soul and I went to the great sea to bathe. And when we reached the shore, we went about looking for a hidden and lonely place.

But as we walked, we saw a man sitting on a grey rock taking pinches of salt from a bag and throwing them into the sea.

"This is the pessimist," said my soul, "Let us leave this place. We cannot bathe here."

We walked on until we reached an inlet. There we saw, standing on a white rock, a man holding a bejeweled box, from which he took sugar and threw it into the sea.

"And this is the optimist," said my soul, "And he too must not see our naked bodies."

Further on we walked. And on a beach we saw a man picking up dead fish and tenderly putting them back into the water.

"And we cannot bathe before him," said my soul. "He is the humane philanthropist."

And we passed on.

Then we came where we saw a man tracing his shadow on the sand. Great waves came and erased it. But he went on tracing it again and again.

"He is the mystic," said my soul, "Let us leave him."

And we walked on, till in a quiet cover we saw a man scooping up the foam and putting it into an alabaster bowl.

"He is the idealist," said my soul, "Surely he must not see our nudity."

And on we walked. Suddenly we heard a voice crying, "This is the sea. This is the deep sea. This is the vast and mighty sea." And when we reached the voice it was a man whose back was turned to the sea, and at his ear he held a shell, listening to its murmur.

And my soul said, "Let us pass on. He is the realist,

who turns his back on the whole he cannot grasp, and busies himself with a fragment."

So we passed on. And in a weedy place among the rocks was a man with his head buried in the sand. And I said to my soul, "We can bath here, for he cannot see us."

"Nay," said my soul, "For he is the most deadly of them all. He is the puritan."

Then a great sadness came over the face of my soul, and into her voice.

"Let us go hence," she said, "For there is no lonely, hidden place where we can bathe. I would not have this wind lift my golden hair, or bare my white bosom in this air, or let the light disclose my sacred nakedness."

Then we left that sea to seek the Greater Sea.

CRUCIFIED

I cried to men, "I would be crucified!"

And they said, "Why should your blood be upon our heads?"

And I answered, "How else shall you be exalted except by crucifying madmen?"

And they heeded and I was crucified. And the crucifixion appeased me.

And when I was hanged between earth and heaven they lifted up their heads to see me. And they were exalted, for their heads had never before been lifted.

But as they stood looking up at me one called out, "For what art thou seeking to atone?"

And another cried, "In what cause dost thou sacrifice thyself?"

And a third said, "Thinkest thou with this price to buy world glory?"

Then said a fourth, "Behold, how he smiles! Can such pain be forgiven?"

And I answered them all, and said:

"Remember only that I smiled. I do not atone—nor sacrifice—nor wish for glory; and I have nothing to forgive. I thirsted—and I besought you to give me my blood to drink. For what is there can quench a madman's thirst but his own blood? I was dumb—and I asked wounds of you for mouths. I was imprisoned in your days and nights—and I sought a door into larger days and nights.

And now I go—as others already crucified have gone. And think not we are weary of crucifixion. For we must be crucified by larger and yet larger men, between greater earths and greater heavens."

THE ASTRONOMER

In the shadow of the temple my friend and I saw a blind man sitting alone. And my friend said, "Behold the wisest man of our land."

Then I left my friend and approached the blind man and greeted him. And we conversed.

After a while I said, "Forgive my question; but since when has thou been blind?"

"From my birth," he answered.

Said I, "And what path of wisdom followest thou?"

Said he, "I am an astronomer."

Then he placed his hand upon his breast saying, "I watch all these suns and moons and stars."

THE GREAT LONGING

Here I sit between my brother the mountain and my sister the sea.

We three are one in loneliness, and the love that binds us together is deep and strong and strange. Nay, it is deeper than my sister's depth and stronger than my brother's strength, and stranger than the strangeness of my madness.

Aeons upon aeons have passed since the first grey dawn made us visible to one another; and though we have seen the birth and the fullness and the death of many worlds, we are still eager and young.

We are young and eager and yet we are mateless and unvisited, and though we lie in unbroken half embrace, we are uncomforted. And what comfort is there for controlled desire and unspent passion? Whence shall come the flaming god to warm my sister's bed? And what she-torrent shall quench my brother's fire? And who is the woman that shall command my heart?

In the stillness of the night my sister murmurs in her sleep the fire-god's unknown name, and my brother calls afar upon the cool and distant goddess. But upon whom I call in my sleep I know not.

Here I sit between my brother the mountain and my sister the sea. We three are one in loneliness, and the love that binds us together is deep and strong and strange.

SAID A BLADE OF GRASS

Said a blade of grass to an autumn leaf, "You make such a noise falling! You scatter all my winter dreams."

Said the leaf indignant, "Low-born and low-dwelling! Songless, peevish thing! You live not in the upper air and you cannot tell the sound of singing."

Then the autumn leaf lay down upon the earth and slept. And when spring came she waked again—and she was a blade of grass.

And when it was autumn and her winter sleep was upon her, and above her through all the air the leaves were falling, she muttered to herself, "O these autumn leaves! They make such noise! They scatter all my winter dreams."

THE EYE

Said the Eye one day, "I see beyond these valleys a mountain veiled with blue mist. Is it not beautiful?"

The Ear listened, and after listening intently awhile, said, "But where is any mountain? I do not hear it."

Then the Hand spoke and said, "I am trying in vain to feel it or touch it, and I can find no mountain."

And the Nose said, "There is no mountain, I cannot smell it."

Then the Eye turned the other way, and they all began to talk together about the Eye's strange delusion. And they said, "Something must be the matter with the Eye."

THE TWO LEARNED MEN

Once there lived in the ancient city of Afkar two learned men who hated and belittled each other's learning.

For one of them denied the existence of the gods and the other was a believer.

One day the two met in the marketplace, and amidst their followers they began to dispute and to argue about the existence or the non-existence of the gods. And after hours of contention they parted.

That evening the unbeliever went to the temple and prostrated himself before the altar and prayed the gods to forgive his wayward past.

And the same hour the other learned man, he who had upheld the gods, burned his sacred books. For he had become an unbeliever.

WHEN MY SORROW WAS BORN

When my Sorrow was born I nursed it with care, and watched over it with loving tenderness.

And my Sorrow grew like all living things, strong and beautiful and full of wondrous delights.

And we loved one another, my Sorrow and I, and we loved the world about us; for Sorrow had a kindly heart and mine was kindly with Sorrow.

And when we conversed, my Sorrow and I, our days were winged and our nights were girdled with dreams; for Sorrow had an eloquent tongue, and mine was eloquent with Sorrow.

And when we sang together, my Sorrow and I, our neighbors sat at their windows and listened; for our songs were deep as the sea and our melodies were full of strange memories.

And when we walked together, my Sorrow and I, people gazed at us with gentle eyes and whispered in words of exceeding sweetness. And there were those who looked with envy upon us, for Sorrow was a noble thing and I was proud with Sorrow.

But my Sorrow died, like all living things, and alone I am left to muse and ponder.

And now when I speak my words fall heavily upon my ears.

And when I sing my songs my neighbours come not to listen.

And when I walk the streets no one looks at me.

Only in my sleep I hear voices saying in pity, "See, there lies the man whose Sorrow is dead."

AND WHEN MY JOY WAS BORN

And when my Joy was born, I held it in my arms and stood on the house-top shouting, "Come ye, my neighbours, come and see, for Joy this day is born unto me. Come and behold this gladsome thing that laugheth in the sun."

But none of my neighbours came to look upon my Joy, and great was my astonishment.

And every day for seven moons I proclaimed my Joy from the house-top—and yet no one heeded me. And my Joy and I were alone, unsought and unvisited.

Then my Joy grew pale and weary because no other heart but mine held its loveliness and no other lips kissed its lips.

Then my Joy died of isolation.

And now I only remember my dead Joy in remembering my dead Sorrow. But memory is an autumn leaf that murmurs a while in the wind and then is heard no more.

"THE PERFECT WORLD"

God of lost souls, thou who are lost amongst the gods, hear me:

Gentle Destiny that watchest over us, mad, wandering spirits, hear me:

I dwell in the midst of a perfect race, I the most imperfect.

I, a human chaos, a nebula of confused elements, I move amongst finished worlds—peoples of complete laws and pure order, whose thoughts are assorted, whose dreams are arranged, and whose visions are enrolled and registered.

Their virtues, O God, are measured, their sins are weighed, and even the countless things that pass in the dim twilight of neither sin nor virtue are recorded and catalogued.

Here days and night are divided into seasons of conduct and governed by rules of blameless accuracy.

To eat, to drink, to sleep, to cover one's nudity, and then to be weary in due time.

To work, to play, to sing, to dance, and then to lie still when the clock strikes the hour.

To think thus, to feel thus much, and then to cease thinking and feeling when a certain star rises above yonder horizon.

To rob a neighbour with a smile, to bestow gifts with a graceful wave of the hand, to praise prudently, to blame cautiously, to destroy a sound with a word, to burn a body with a breath, and then to wash the hands when the day's work is done.

To love according to an established order, to entertain one's best self in a preconceived manner, to worship the gods becomingly, to intrigue the devils artfully—and then to forget all as though memory were dead.

To fancy with a motive, to contemplate with consideration, to be happy sweetly, to suffer nobly—and then to empty the cup so that tomorrow may fill it again.

All these things, O God, are conceived with forethought, born with determination, nursed with exactness, governed by rules, directed by reason, and then slain and buried after a prescribed method. And even their silent graves that lie within the human soul are marked and numbered.

It is a perfect world, a world of consummate excellence, a world of supreme wonders, the ripest fruit in God's garden, the master-thought of the universe.

But why should I be here, O God, I a green seed of unfulfilled passion, a mad tempest that seeketh neither east nor west, a bewildered fragment from a burnt planet?

Why am I here, O God of lost souls, thou who art lost amongst the gods?

THE FORERUNNER
HIS PARABLES AND POEMS

You are your own forerunner, and the towers you have builded are but the foundation of your giant-self. And that self too shall be a foundation.

And I too am my own forerunner, for the long shadow stretching before me at sunrise shall gather under my feet at the noon hour. Yet another sunrise shall lay another shadow before me, and that also shall be gathered at another noon.

Always have we been our own forerunners, and always shall we be. And all that we have gathered and shall gather shall be but seeds for fields yet unploughed. We are the fields and the ploughmen, the gatherers and the gathered.

When you were a wandering desire in the mist, I too was there, a wandering desire. Then we sought one another, and out of our eagerness dreams were born. And dreams were time limitless, and dreams were space without measure.

And when you were a silent word upon Life's quivering lips, I too was there, another silent word. Then Life uttered us and we came down the years throbbing with memories of yesterday and with longing for tomorrow, for yesterday was death conquered and tomorrow was birth pursued.

And now we are in God's hands. You are a sun in His right hand and I an earth in His left hand. Yet you are not more, shining, than I, shone upon.

And we, sun and earth, are but the beginning of a greater sun and a greater earth. And always shall we be the beginning.

*****

You are your own forerunner, you the stranger passing by the gate of my garden.

And I too am my own forerunner, though I sit in the shadows of my trees and seem motionless.

GOD'S FOOL

ONCE there came from the desert to the great city of Sharia a man who was a dreamer, and he had naught but his garment and a staff.

And as he walked through the streets he gazed with awe and wonder at the temples and towers and palaces, for the city of Sharia was of surpassing beauty. And he spoke often to the passersby, questioning them about their city—but they understood not his language, nor he their language.

At the noon hour he stopped before a vast inn. It was built of yellow marble, and people were going in and coming out unhindered.

"This must be a shrine," he said to himself, and he too went in. But what was his surprise to find himself in a hall of great splendour and a large company of men and women seated about many tables. They were eating and drinking and listening to the musicians.

"Nay," said the dreamer. "This is no worshipping. It must be a feast given by the prince to the people, in celebration of a great event."

At that moment a man, whom he took to be the slave of the prince, approached him, and bade him be seated. And he was served with meat and wine and most excellent sweets.

When he was satisfied, the dreamer rose to depart. At the door he was stopped by a large man magnificently arrayed.

"Surely this is the prince himself," said the dreamer in his heart, and he bowed to him and thanked him.

Then the large man said in the language of the city:

"Sir, you have not paid for your dinner." And the dreamer did not understand, and again thanked him heartily. Then the large man bethought him, and he looked more closely upon the dreamer. And he saw that he was a stranger, clad in but a poor garment, and that indeed he had not wherewith to pay for his meal. Then the large man clapped his hands and called—and there came four watchmen of the city. And they listened to the large man. Then they took the dreamer between them, and they were two on each side of him. And the dreamer noted the ceremoniousness of their dress and of their manner and he looked upon them with delight.

"These," said he, "are men of distinction."

And they walked all together until they came to the House of Judgment and they entered.

The dreamer saw before him, seated upon a throne, a venerable man with flowing beard, robed majestically. And he thought he was the king. And he rejoiced to be brought before him.

Now the watchmen related to the judge, who was the venerable man, the charge against the dreamer; and the judge appointed two advocates, one to present the charge and the other to defend the stranger. And the advocates rose, the one after the other, and delivered each his argument. And the dreamer thought himself to be listening to addresses of welcome, and his heart filled with gratitude to the king and the prince for all that was done for him.

Then sentence was passed upon the dreamer, that upon a tablet hung about his neck his crime should be written, and that he should ride through the city on a naked horse, with a trumpeter and a drummer before him. And the sentence was carried out forthwith.

Now as the dreamer rode through the city upon the naked horse, with the trumpeter and the drummer before him, the inhabitants of the city came running forth at the sound of the noise, and when they saw him they laughed one and all, and the children ran after him in companies from street to street. And the dreamer's heart was filled with ecstasy, and his eyes shone upon them. For to him the tablet was a sign of the king's blessing and the procession was in his honour.

Now as he rode, he saw among the crowd a man who was from the desert like himself and his heart swelled with joy, and he cried out to him with a shout:

"Friend! Friend! Where are we? What city of the heart's desire is this? What race of lavish hosts?—who feast the chance guest in their palaces, whose princes companion him, whose king hangs a token upon his breast and opens to him the hospitality of a city descended from heaven."

And he who was also of the desert replied not. He only smiled and slightly shook his head. And the procession passed on.

And the dreamer's face was uplifted and his eyes were overflowing with light.

LOVE

They say the jackal and the mole
Drink from the self-same stream
Where the lion comes to drink.

And they say the eagle and the vulture
Dig their beaks into the same carcass,
And are at peace, one with the other,
In the presence of the dead thing.

O love, whose lordly hand
Has bridled my desires,
And raised my hunger and my thirst
To dignity and pride,
Let not the strong in me and the constant
Eat the bread or drink the wine
That tempt my weaker self.
Let me rather starve,
And let my heart parch with thirst,
And let me die and perish,
Ere I stretch my hand
To a cup you did not fill,
Or a bowl you did not bless.

THE KING-HERMIT

THEY told me that in a forest among the mountains lives a young man in solitude who once was a king of a vast country beyond the Two Rivers. And they also said that he, of his own will, had left his throne and the land of his glory and come to dwell in the wilderness.

And I said, "I would seek that man, and learn the secret of his heart; for he who renounces a kingdom must needs be greater than a kingdom."

On that very day I went to the forest where he dwells. And I found him sitting under a white cypress, and in his hand a reed as if it were a sceptre. And I greeted him even as I would greet a king.

And he turned to me and said gently, "What would you in this forest of serenity? Seek you a lost self in the green shadows, or is it a home-coming in your twilight?"

And I answered, "I sought but you—for I fain would know that which made you leave a kingdom for a forest."

And he said, "Brief is my story, for sudden was the bursting of the bubble. It happened thus: One day as I sat at a window in my palace, my chamberlain and an envoy from a foreign land were walking in my garden. And as they approached my window, the lord chamberlain was speaking of himself and saying, 'I am like the king; I have a thirst for strong wine and a hunger for all games of chance. And like my lord the king I have storms of temper.' And the lord chamberlain and the envoy disappeared among the trees. But in a few minutes they returned, and this time the lord chamberlain was speaking of me, and he was saying, 'My lord the king is like myself—a good marksman; and like me he loves music and bathes thrice a day.'"

After a moment he added, "On the eve of that day I left my palace with but my garment, for I would no longer be ruler over those who assume my vices and attribute to me their virtues."

And I said, "This is indeed a wonder, and passing strange."

And he said, "Nay, my friend, you knocked at the gate of my silences and received but a trifle. For who would not leave a kingdom for a forest where the seasons sing and dance ceaselessly? Many are those who have given their kingdom for less than solitude and the sweet fellowship of aloneness. Countless are the eagles who descend from the upper air to live with moles that they may know the secrets of the earth. There are those who renounce the kingdom of dreams that they may not seem distant from the dreamless. And those who renounce the kingdom of nakedness and cover their souls that others may not be ashamed in beholding truth uncovered and beauty unveiled. And greater yet than all of these is he who renounces the kingdom of sorrow that he may not seem proud and vainglorious."

Then rising he leaned upon his reed and said, "Go now to the great city and sit at its gate and watch all those who enter into it and those who go out. And see that you find him who, though born a king, is without kingdom; and him who though ruled in flesh rules in spirit—though neither he nor his subjects know this; and him also who but seems to rule yet is in truth slave of his own slaves."

After he had said these things he smiled on me, and there were a thousand dawns upon his lips. Then he turned and walked away into the heart of the forest.

And I returned to the city, and I sat at its gate to watch the passersby even as he had told me. And from that day to this numberless are the kings whose shadows have passed over me and few are the subjects over whom my shadow has passed.

THE LION'S DAUGHTER

FOUR slaves stood fanning an old queen who was asleep upon her throne. And she was snoring. And upon the queen's lap a cat lay purring and gazing lazily at the slaves.

The first slave spoke, and said, "How ugly this old woman is in her sleep. See her mouth droop; and she breathes as if the devil were choking her."

Then the cat said, purring, "Not half so ugly in her sleep as you in your waking slavery."

And the second slave said, "You would think sleep would smooth her wrinkles instead of deepening them. She must be dreaming of something evil."

And the cat purred, "Would that you might sleep also and dream of your freedom."

And the third slave said, "Perhaps she is seeing the procession of all those that she has slain."

And the cat purred, "Aye, she sees the procession of your forefathers and your descendants."

And the fourth slave said, "It is all very well to talk about her, but it does not make me less weary of standing and fanning."

And the cat purred, "You shall be fanning to all eternity; for as it is on earth so it is in heaven."

At this moment the old queen nodded in her sleep, and her crown fell to the floor.

And one of the slaves said, "That is a bad omen."

And the cat purred, "The bad omen of one is the good omen of another."

And the second slave said, "What if she should wake, and find her crown fallen! She would surely slay us."

And the cat purred, "Daily from your birth she has slain you and you know it not."

And the third slave said, "Yes, she would slay us and she would call it making sacrifice to the gods."

And the cat purred, "Only the weak are sacrificed to the gods."

And the fourth slave silenced the others, and softly he picked up the crown and replaced it, without waking her, on the old queen's head.

And the cat purred, "Only a slave restores a crown that has fallen."

And after a while the old queen woke, and she looked about her and yawned. Then she said, "Methought I dreamed, and I saw four caterpillars chased by a scorpion around the trunk of an ancient oaktree. I like not my dream."

Then she closed her eyes and went to sleep again. And she snored. And the four slaves went on fanning her.

And the cat purred, "Fan on, fan on, stupids. You fan but the fire that consumes you."

TYRANNY

THUS sings the She-Dragon that guards the seven caves by the sea:

"My mate shall come riding on the waves. His thundering roar shall fill the earth with fear, and the flames of his nostrils shall set the sky afire. At the eclipse of the moon we shall be wedded, and at the eclipse of the sun I shall give birth to a Saint George, who shall slay me."

Thus sings the She-Dragon that guards the seven caves by the sea.

THE SAINT

IN my youth I once visited a saint in his silent grove beyond the hills; and as we were conversing upon the nature of virtue a brigand came limping wearily up the ridge. When he reached the grove he knelt down before the saint and said, "O saint, I would be comforted! My sins are heavy upon me."

And the saint replied, "My sins, too, are heavy upon me."

And the brigand said, "But I am a thief and a plunderer."

And the saint replied, "I too am a thief and a plunderer."

And the brigand said, "But I am a murderer, and the blood of many men cries in my ears."

And the saint replied, "I too am a murderer, and in my ears cries the blood of many men."

And the brigand said, "I have committed countless crimes."

And the saint replied, "I too have committed crimes without number."

Then the brigand stood up and gazed at the saint, and there was a strange look in his eyes. And when he left us he went skipping down the hill.

And I turned to the saint and said, "Wherefore did you accuse yourself of uncommitted crimes? See you not that this man went away no longer believing in you?"

And the saint answered, "It is true he no longer believes in me. But he went away much comforted."

At that moment we heard the brigand singing in the distance, and the echo of his song filled the valley with gladness.

THE PLUTOCRAT

IN my wanderings I once saw upon an island a man-headed, iron-hoofed monster who ate of the earth and drank of the sea incessantly. And for a long while I watched him. Then I approached him and said, "Have you never enough; is your hunger never satisfied and your thirst never quenched?"

And he answered saying, "Yes, I am satisfied, nay, I am weary of eating and drinking; but I am afraid that tomorrow there will be no more earth to eat and no more sea to drink."

THE GREATER SELF

THIS came to pass. After the coronation of Nufsibaäl, King of Byblus, he retired to his bed chamber—the very room which the three hermit-magicians of the mountain had built for him. He took off his crown and his royal raiment, and stood in the centre of the room thinking of himself, now the all-powerful ruler of Byblus.

Suddenly he turned; and he saw stepping out of the silver mirror which his mother had given him, a naked man.

The king was startled, and he cried out to the man, "What would you?"

And the naked man answered, "Naught but this: Why have they crowned you king?"

And the king answered, "Because I am the noblest man in the land."

Then the naked man said, "If you were still more noble, you would not be king."

And the king said, "Because I am the mightiest man in the land they crowned me."

And the naked man said, "If you were mightier yet, you would not be king."

Then the king said, "Because I am the wisest man they crowned me king."

And the naked man said, "If you were still wiser you would not choose to be king."

Then the king fell to the floor and wept bitterly.

The naked man looked down upon him. Then he took up the crown and with tenderness replaced it upon the king's bent head.

And the naked man, gazing lovingly upon the king, entered into the mirror.

And the king roused, and straightway he looked into the mirror. And he saw there but himself crowned.

WAR AND THE SMALL NATIONS

ONCE, high above a pasture, where a sheep and a lamb were grazing, an eagle was circling and gazing hungrily down upon the lamb. And as he was about to descend and seize his prey, another eagle appeared and hovered above the sheep and her young with the same hungry intent. Then the two rivals began to fight filling the sky with their fierce cries.

The sheep looked up and was much astonished. She turned to the lamb and said,

"How strange, my child, that these two noble birds should attack one another. Is not the vast sky large enough for both of them? Pray, my little one, pray in your heart that God may make peace between your winged brothers."

And the lamb prayed in his heart.

ONE nightfall a man travelling on horseback toward the sea reached an inn by the roadside. He dismounted, and confident in man and night like all riders toward the sea, he tied his horse to a tree beside the door and entered into the inn.

At midnight, when all were asleep, a thief came and stole the traveller's horse.

In the morning the man awoke, and discovered that his horse was stolen. And he grieved for his horse, and that a man had found it in his heart to steal.

Then his fellow-lodgers came and stood around him and began to talk.

And the first man said, "How foolish of you to tie your horse outside the stable."

And the second said, "Still more foolish, without even hobbling the horse!"

And the third man said, "It is stupid at best to travel to the sea on horseback."

And the fourth said, "Only the indolent and the slow of foot own horses."

Then the traveller was much astonished. At last he cried, "My friends, because my horse is stolen, you have hastened one and all to tell me my faults and my shortcomings. But strange, not one word of reproach have you uttered about the man who stole my horse."

POETS

FOUR poets were sitting around a bowl of punch that stood on a table.

Said the first poet, "Methinks I see with my third eye the fragrance of this wine hovering in space like a cloud of birds in an enchanted forest."

The second poet raised his head and said, "With my inner ear I can hear those mist-birds singing. And the melody holds my heart as the white rose imprisons the bee within her petals."

The third poet closed his eyes and stretched his arm upward, and said, "I touch them with my hand. I feel their wings, like the breath of a sleeping fairy, brushing against my fingers."

Then the fourth poet rose and lifted up the bowl, and he said, "Alas, friends! I am too dull of sight and of hearing and of touch. I cannot see the fragrance of this wine, nor hear its song, nor feel the beating of its wings. I perceive but the wine itself. Now therefore must I drink it, that it may sharpen my senses and raise me to your blissful heights."

And putting the bowl to his lips, he drank the punch to the very last drop.

The three poets, with their mouths open, looked at him aghast, and there was a thirsty yet unlyrical hatred in their eyes.

THE WEATHER-COCK

SAID the weather-cock to the wind, "How tedious and monotonous you are! Can you not blow any other way but in my face? You disturb my God-given stability."

And the wind did not answer. It only laughed in space.

ONCE the elders of the city of Aradus presented themselves before the king, and besought of him a decree to forbid to men all wine and all intoxicants within their city.

And the king turned his back upon them and went out from them laughing.

Then the elders departed in dismay.

At the door of the palace they met the lord chamberlain. And the lord chamberlain observed that they were troubled, and he understood their case.

Then he said, "Pity, my friends! Had you found the king drunk, surely he would have granted you your petition."

OUT OF MY DEEPER HEART

OUT of my deeper heart a bird rose and flew skyward.

Higher and higher did it rise, yet larger and larger did it grow.

At first it was but like a swallow, then a lark, then an eagle, then as vast as a spring cloud, and then it filled the starry heavens.

Out of my heart a bird flew skyward. And it waxed larger as it flew. Yet it left not my heart.

*****

O my faith, my untamed knowledge, how shall I fly to your height and see with you man's larger self pencilled upon the sky?

How shall I turn this sea within me into mist, and move with you in space immeasurable?

How can a prisoner within the temple behold its golden domes?

How shall the heart of a fruit be stretched to envelop the fruit also?

O my faith, I am in chains behind these bars of silver and ebony, and I cannot fly with you.

Yet out of my heart you rise skyward, and it is my heart that holds you, and I shall be content.

DYNASTIES

THE Queen of Ishana was in travail of childbirth; and the King and the mighty men of his court were waiting in breathless anxiety in the great hall of the Winged Bulls.

At eventide there came suddenly a messenger in haste and prostrated himself before the King, and said, "I bring glad tidings unto my lord the King, and unto the kingdom and the slaves of the King. Mihrab the Cruel, thy life-long enemy, the King of Bethroun, is dead."

When the King and the mighty men heard this, they all rose and shouted for joy; for the powerful Mihrab, had he lived longer, had assuredly overcome Ishana and carried the inhabitants captive.

At this moment the court physician also entered the hall of Winged Bulls, and behind him came the royal midwives. And the physician prostrated himself before the king, and said, "My lord the King shall live for ever, and through countless generations shall he rule over the people of Ishana. For unto thee, O King, is born this very hour a son, who shall be thy heir."

Then indeed was the soul of the King intoxicated with joy, that in the same moment his foe was dead and the royal line was established.

Now in the City of Ishana lived a true prophet. And the prophet was young, and bold of spirit. And the King that very night ordered that the prophet should be brought before him. And when he was brought, the King said unto him, "Prophesy now, and foretell what shall be the future of my son who is this day born unto the kingdom."

And the prophet hesitated not, but said, "Hearken, O King, and I will indeed prophesy of the future of thy son, that is this day born. The soul of thy enemy, even of thy enemy King Mihrab, who died yestereve, lingered but a day upon the wind. Then it sought for itself a body to enter into. And that which it entered into was the body of thy son that, is born unto thee this hour."

Then the King was enraged, and with his sword he slew the prophet.

And from that day to this, the wise men of Ishana say one to another secretly, "Is it not known, and has it not been said from of old, that Ishana is ruled by an enemy."

KNOWLEDGE AND HALF-KNOWLEDGE

FOUR frogs sat upon a log that lay floating on the edge of a river. Suddenly the log was caught by the current and swept slowly down the stream. The frogs were delighted and absorbed, for never before had they sailed.

At length the first frog spoke, and said, "This is indeed a most marvellous log. It moves as if alive. No such log was ever known before."

Then the second frog spoke, and said, "Nay, my friend, the log is like other logs, and does not move. It is the river, that is walking to the sea, and carries us and the log with it."

And the third frog spoke, and said, "It is neither the log nor the river that moves. The moving is in our thinking. For without thought nothing moves."

And the three frogs began to wrangle about what was really moving. The quarrel grew hotter and louder, but they could not agree.

Then they turned to the fourth frog, who up to this time had been listening attentively but holding his peace, and they asked his opinion.

And the fourth frog said, "Each of you is right, and none of you is wrong. The moving is in the log and the water and our thinking also."

And the three frogs became very angry, for none of them was willing to admit that his was not the whole truth, and that the other two were not wholly wrong.

Then the strange thing happened. The three frogs got together and pushed the fourth frog off the log into the river.

"SAID A SHEET OF SNOW-WHITE PAPER...."

SAID a sheet of snow-white paper, "Pure was I created, and pure will I remain for ever. I would rather be burnt and turn to white ashes than suffer darkness to touch me or the unclean to come near me."

The ink-bottle heard what the paper was saying, and it laughed in its dark heart; but it never dared to approach her. And the multicoloured pencils heard her also, and they too never came near her.

And the snow-white sheet of paper did remain pure and chaste for ever—pure and chaste—and empty.

SAID the serpent to the lark, "Thou flyest, yet thou canst not visit the recesses of the earth where the sap of life moveth in perfect silence."

And the lark answered, "Aye, thou knowest over much, nay thou art wiser than all things wise—pity thou canst not fly."

And as if he did not hear, the serpent said, "Thou canst not see the secrets of the deep, nor move among the treasures of the hidden empire. It was but yesterday I lay in a cave of rubies. It is like the heart of a ripe pomegranate, and the faintest ray of light turns it into a flame-rose. Who but me can behold such marvels?"

And the lark said, "None, none but thee can lie among the crystal memories of the cycles: pity thou canst not sing."

And the serpent said, "I know a plant whose root descends to the bowels of the earth, and he who eats of that root becomes fairer than Ashtarte."

And the lark said, "No one, no one but thee could unveil the magic thought of the earth—pity thou canst not fly."

And the serpent said, "There is a purple stream that runneth under a mountain, and he who drinketh of it shall become immortal even as the gods. Surely no bird or beast can discover that purple stream."

And the lark answered, "If thou willest thou canst become deathless even as the gods—pity thou canst not sing."

And the serpent said, "I know a buried temple, which I visit once a moon: It was built by a forgotten race of giants, and upon its walls are graven the secrets of time and space, and he who reads them shall understand that which passeth all understanding."

And the lark said, "Verily, if thou so desirest thou canst encircle with thy pliant body all knowledge of time and space—pity thou canst not fly."

Then the serpent was disgusted, and as he turned and entered into his hole he muttered, "Empty headed songster!"

And the lark flew away singing, "Pity thou canst not sing. Pity, pity, my wise one, thou canst not fly."

VALUES

ONCE a man unearthed in his field a marble statue of great beauty. And he took it to a collector who loved all beautiful things and offered it to him for sale, and the collector bought it for a large price. And they parted.

And as the man walked home with his money he thought, and he said to himself, "How much life this money means! How can any one give all this for a dead carved stone buried and undreamed of in the earth for a thousand years?"

And now the collector was looking at his statue, and he was thinking, and he said to himself, "What beauty! What life! The dream of what a soul!—and fresh with the sweet sleep of a thousand years. How can any one give all this for money, dead and dreamless?"

OTHER SEAS

A FISH said to another fish, "Above this sea of ours there is another sea, with creatures swimming in it—and they live there even as we live here."

The fish replied, "Pure fancy! Pure fancy! When you know that everything that leaves our sea by even an inch, and stays out of it, dies. What proof have you of other lives in other seas?"

REPENTANCE

ON a moonless night a man entered into his neighbour's garden and stole the largest melon he could find and brought it home.

He opened it and found it still unripe.

Then behold a marvel!

The man's conscience woke and smote him with remorse; and he repented having stolen the melon.

THE DYING MAN AND THE VULTURE

Wait, wait yet awhile, my eager friend.
I shall yield but too soon this wasted thing,
Whose agony overwrought and useless
Exhausts your patience.
I would not have your honest hunger
Wait upon these moments:
But this chain, though made of a breath,
Is hard to break.
And the will to die,
Stronger than all things strong,
Is stayed by a will to live
Feebler than all things feeble.
Forgive me comrade; I tarry too long.
It is memory that holds my spirit;
A procession of distant days,
A vision of youth spent in a dream,
A face that bids my eyelids not to sleep,
A voice that lingers in my ears,
A hand that touches my hand.
Forgive me that you have waited too long.
It is over now, and all is faded:—
The face, the voice, the hand and the mist
that brought them hither.
The knot is untied.
The cord is cleaved.
And that which is neither food nor drink is withdrawn.
Approach, my hungry comrade;
The board is made ready,
And the fare, frugal and spare,
Is given with love.
Come, and dig your beak here, into the left side,
And tear out of its cage this smaller bird,

Whose wings can beat no more:
I would have it soar with you into the sky.
Come now, my friend, I am your host tonight,
And you my welcome guest.

BEYOND MY SOLITUDE

BEYOND my solitude is another solitude, and to him who dwells therein my aloneness is a crowded marketplace and my silence a confusion of sounds.

Too young am I and too restless to seek that above-solitude. The voices of yonder valley still hold my ears, and its shadows bar my way and I cannot go.

Beyond these hills is a grove of enchantment and to him who dwells therein my peace is but a whirlwind and my enchantment an illusion.

Too young am I and too riotous to seek that sacred grove. The taste of blood is clinging in my mouth, and the bow and the arrows of my fathers yet linger in my hand and I cannot go.

Beyond this burdened self lives my freer self; and to him my dreams are a battle fought in twilight and my desires the rattling of bones.

Too young am I and too outraged to be my freer self.

And how shall I become my freer self unless I slay my burdened selves, or unless all men become free?

How shall my leaves fly singing upon the wind unless my roots shall wither in the dark?

How shall the eagle in me soar against the sun until my fledglings leave the nest which I with my own beak have built for them?

THE LAST WATCH

AT the high-tide of night, when the first breath of dawn came upon the wind, the Forerunner, he who calls himself echo to a voice yet unheard, left his bed-chamber and ascended to the roof of his house. Long he stood and looked down upon the slumbering city. Then he raised his head, and even as if the sleepless spirits of all those asleep had gathered around him, he opened his lips and spoke, and he said:

"My friends and my neighbours and you who daily pass my gate, I would speak to you in your sleep, and in the valley of your dreams I would walk naked and unrestrained; far heedless are your waking hours and deaf are your sound-burdened ears.

"Long did I love you and overmuch.

"I love the one among you as though he were all, and all as if you were one. And in the spring of my heart I sang in your gardens, and in the summer of my heart I watched at your threshing-floors.

"Yea, I loved you all, the giant and the pigmy, the leper and the anointed, and him who gropes in the dark even as him who dances his days upon the mountains.

"You, the strong, have I loved, though the marks of your iron hoofs are yet upon my flesh; and you the weak, though you have drained my faith and wasted my patience.

"You the rich have I loved, while bitter was your honey to my mouth; and you the poor, though you knew my empty-handed shame.

"You the poet with the barrowed lute and blind fingers, you have I loved in self indulgence; and you the scholar, ever gathering rotted shrouds in potters' fields.

"You the priest I have loved, who sit in the silences of yesterday questioning the fate of my tomorrow; and you the worshippers of gods the images of your own desires.

"You the thirsting woman whose cup is ever full, I have loved you in understanding; and you the woman of restless nights, you too I have loved in pity.

"You the talkative have I loved, saying, 'Life hath much to say'; and you the dumb have I loved, whispering to myself, 'Says he not in silence that which I fain would hear in words?'

"And you the judge and the critic, I have loved also; yet when you have seen me crucified, you said, 'He bleeds rhythmically, and the pattern his blood makes upon his white skin is beautiful to behold.'

"Yea, I have loved you all, the young and the old, the trembling reed and the oak.

"But alas! it was the over-abundance of my heart that turned you from me. You would drink love from a cup, but not from a surging river. You would hear love's faint murmur, but when love shouts you would muffle your ears.

"And because I have loved you all you have said, 'Too soft and yielding is his heart, and too undiscerning is his path. It is the love of a needy one, who picks crumbs even as he sits at kingly feasts. And it is the love of a weakling, for the strong loves only the strong.'

"And because I have loved you overmuch you have said, 'It is but the love of a blind man who knows not the beauty of one nor the ugliness of another. And it is the love of the tasteless who drinks vinegar even as wine. And it is the love of the impertinent and the overweening, for what stranger could be our mother and father and sister and brother?'

"This you have said, and more. For often in the marketplace you pointed your fingers at me and said mockingly, 'There goes the ageless one, the man without seasons, who at the noon hour plays games with our children and at eventide sits with our elders and assumes wisdom and understanding.'

"And I said 'I will love them more. Aye, even more. I will hide my love with seeming to hate, and disguise my tenderness as bitterness. I will wear an iron mask, and only when armed and mailed shall I seek them.'

"Then I laid a heavy hand upon your bruises, and like a tempest in the night I thundered in your ears.

"From the housetop I proclaimed you hypocrites, pharisees, tricksters, false and empty earth-bubbles.

"The short-sighted among you I cursed for blind bats, and those too near the earth I likened to soulless moles.

"The eloquent I pronounced fork-tongued, the silent, stone-lipped, and the simple and artless I called the dead never weary of death.

"The seekers after world knowledge I condemned as offenders of the holy spirit and those who would naught but the spirit I branded as hunters of shadows who cast their nets in flat waters and catch but their own images.

"Thus with my lips have I denounced you, while my heart, bleeding within me, called you tender names.

"It was love lashed by its own self that spoke. It was pride half slain that fluttered in the dust. It was my hunger for your love that raged from the housetop, while my own love, kneeling in silence, prayed your forgiveness.

"But behold a miracle!

"It was my disguise that opened your eyes, and my seeming to hate that woke your hearts.

"And now you love me.

"You love the swords that strike you and the arrows that crave your breast. For it comforts you to be wounded and only when you drink of your own blood can you be intoxicated.

"Like moths that seek destruction in the flame you gather daily in my garden: and with faces uplifted and eyes enchanted you watch me tear the fabric of your days.

And in whispers you say the one to the other, 'He sees with the light of God. He speaks like the prophets of old. He unveils our souls and unlocks our hearts, and like the eagle that knows the way of foxes he knows our ways.'

"Aye, in truth, I know your ways, but only as an eagle knows the ways of his fledglings. And I fain would disclose my secret. Yet in my need for your nearness I feign remoteness, and in fear of the ebbtide of your love I guard the floodgates of my love."

After saying these things the Forerunner covered his face with his hands and wept bitterly. For he knew in his heart that love humiliated in its nakedness is greater than love that seeks triumph in disguise; and he was ashamed.

But suddenly he raised his head, and like one waking from sleep he outstretched his arms and said, "Night is over, and we children of night must die when dawn comes leaping upon the hills; and out of our ashes a mightier love shall rise. And it shall laugh in the sun, and it shall be deathless."

THE END